T0068211

Nothing
but
Greatness

AFFIRMATIONS FOR WOMEN

Constance Ne'Cole Johnson

WESTBOW
PRESS®
A DIVISION OF THOMAS NELSON
& ZONDERVAN

WestBow Press books may be ordered through booksellers or by contacting:

WestBow Press
A Division of Thomas Nelson & Zondervan
1663 Liberty Drive
Bloomington, IN 47403
www.westbowpress.com
844-714-3454

Because of the dynamic nature of the Internet, any web addresses or links contained in this book may have changed since publication and may no longer be valid. The views expressed in this work are solely those of the author and do not necessarily reflect the views of the publisher, and the publisher hereby disclaims any responsibility for them.

Any people depicted in stock imagery provided by Getty Images are models, and such images are being used for illustrative purposes only. Certain stock imagery © Getty Images.

Scripture marked (NKJV) taken from the New King James Version®. Copyright © 1982 by Thomas Nelson. Used by permission. All rights reserved.

Scripture quotations marked (NIV) are taken from the Holy Bible, New International Version®, NIV®. Copyright © 1973, 1978, 1984, 2011 by Biblica, Inc.® Used by permission of Zondervan. All rights reserved worldwide. www.zondervan. com The "NIV" and "New International Version" are trademarks registered in the United States Patent and Trademark Office by Biblica, Inc.®

Scripture marked (KJV) taken from the King James Version of the Bible.

Scripture quotations marked (NLT) are taken from the Holy Bible, New Living Translation, copyright ©1996, 2004, 2015 by Tyndale House Foundation. Used by permission of Tyndale House Publishers, Carol Stream, Illinois 60188. All rights reserved.

Scripture quotations marked CSB have been taken from the Christian Standard Bible®, Copyright © 2017 by Holman Bible Publishers. Used by permission. Christian Standard Bible® and CSB® are federally registered trademarks of Holman Bible Publishers.

ISBN: 978-1-6642-3353-9 (sc)
ISBN: 978-1-6642-3354-6 (e)

Library of Congress Control Number: 2021909213

Print information available on the last page.

WestBow Press rev. date: 05/20/2021

This book is dedicated to my mother, father and siblings. When I was growing up, I always wondered why my mom was so hard on my siblings and me, and it was not until I got older that I understood she wanted nothing but the best for us. Ma, I appreciate all you have done for me throughout the years. I love you *always!*

Daddy, although you are not here with me physically, you are always here in spirit. Not a day goes by that I do not think about you. The memories will forever be in my heart. I miss and love you dearly. Your one and only!

To my sister and brother, no matter what obstacles are thrown our way, just know that I love you both no matter what. I love y'all!

Contents

Introduction

Growing up in Decatur, Georgia, I have always been a believer in Christ. My family and I would go to church every Sunday and Wednesday for Bible study. When I got to high school, that is when attending church declined. After high school, I went on to college, where I was not focused due to me being in the "crowd" and in a relationship. I was more focused on the relationship than I was on school. The relationship lasted six years, and I was finding myself putting everyone's needs before my own. I never really had a chance to be by myself, which led me to make decisions on my own instead of seeking God.

Thinking my way was the best way when God's way is better.

As I got older, I started attending church on and off again; however, I would only pray when things got rough. After the relationship ended, I joined a church where I understood everything the pastor would preach about, and it always seem as if he were speaking directly to me. I looked forward to going to church every Sunday.

When I got back into a relationship, attending church declined again. As the years went by, I was not attending church every Sunday, and there was no excuse for it. I was putting the relationship before God, which caused me again to make decisions without seeking God first.

Throughout the years, I experienced life's ups and downs. I would go to friends and family every time I had an issue instead of talking to God. Talking to friends is OK at times, but only God has the answers to our situations.

When coronavirus took over our nation, I was in quarantine working from home. I began to watch my church service online faithfully every

Sunday. I would also watch other pastors' sermons and spiritual messages that were uplifting. Being at home every day allowed me to think about everything from personal to work life.

At the time, I was engaged; however, I was not at peace with where my life was. My emotions were all over the place, and I had the worst attitude. I was not my best; therefore, I could not give my best. What I thought I wanted in my life, which were marriage and kids, I really was not ready for, and God had other plans. I would always worry about what others would say or think about the decisions I would make. It appeared I needed validation and confirmation from others to make decisions; however, God has the answers when you diligently seek Him.

Oftentimes, we point the finger at the other person not to say they did not do anything wrong but do not take the time to self-reflect on self to see why we continue to allow certain situations to happen.

I remember listening to "Something Has to Break" by Kierra Sheard one day and started crying out to God that something must change in my life. I was emotionally drained and felt like I had lost myself. I would paint a picture that everything was OK, but it really was not as I really wanted everything to be OK. I began to pray and asked God, "Where do You want me in this season?" This was the very beginning of starting my spiritual journey, and I had no idea where God was going to lead me; however, I was putting my faith and trust in Him.

God's promises to never leave or forsake us. I began reading God's Word in addition to watching spiritual messages and started speaking affirmations over my life daily and praying God's word back to Him, which is the most powerful way to pray.

My life changed for the better when I made the decision to make God a priority in my life and step out on faith.

Walking away from the relationship allowed me to change my mindset and outlook on life and to become the best version of myself. I was finally at peace and happy. In building my relationship with God, I was no longer interested in things I loved doing. God had me in isolation, in which he had my undivided attention. Change did not happen overnight; however, I knew I made the best decision for myself. I knew that God was with me the entire time, even though I could not hear His voice clearly when He was speaking. I made a commitment not to start or end my day without spending time with God; I was reading the Bible and journaling. The more I would study the word, the more God was pouring blessings into my life.

I yearned to hear God's voice clearly, so I decided to fast and pray for thirty-one days. I pushed my way through! Four days after I completed fasting, God gave me the vision to write a book. I did not know where to begin, but I trusted that the visions I was given would come to fruition. The affirmations and Bible verses are things I do daily to grow my relationship with God. Therefore, I decided to write and publish the affirmation book along with incorporating the scriptures that would help and encourage women to speak *nothing but greatness* over their lives and to get their fight back. Women are powerful and can accomplish anything. Everything in this book helped me to become a better person.

In completing the book, I noticed the number thirty-one popped into my head, and I began to read Proverbs 31. Proverbs 31 talks about being a virtuous woman, and although we as women are not perfect, God does not expect us to be perfect. God desires for us to honor Him in all our ways.

The scriptures in this book helped me to move forward in my faith in God. If it were not for God's grace and mercy, I do not know where I would be. I did not see change overnight; however, I knew I did not want anything but what God had for me, so I promised God that I would make Him a priority no matter what.

I can honestly say making Him a priority was the best decision ever. Prayer changes things!

God first.

Prayer

Heavenly Father,

I pray that every woman who receives and reads this book and speaks the positive affirmations will be healed and blessed. Lord God, allow them to seek You in every area of their life. We know that everything works together for the good of those who love You. Lord, fill each woman up with Your wisdom, strength, courage, peace, power, and boldness. Make her whole, and have Your way in her life, oh God. Allow her to let go of anything or anyone that is hindering her from moving forward into the divine purpose You have for her life. We pull down and rebuke every stronghold, evil spirit, evil thought, and wandering mind that has come over every woman reading this book, and we plead the blood of Jesus. Let no weapon formed against her prosper. Lord God, we are putting our trust and faith in You that You will continue to lead and guide us. Thank You for Your grace and mercy as Your grace is sufficient, oh God. We decree and declare the best is yet to come.

In the mighty name of Jesus, amen.

I am blessed ...

Blessed is she who believed, for there will be a fulfillment
of those things which were told to her from the Lord.

—Luke 1:45 (NKJV)

We are blessed no matter what our lives look like. Whether we have
everything we want or need, we are blessed to see another day.

I am grateful ...

Be anxious for nothing, but in everything by prayer and supplication, with thanksgiving, let your request be made known to God.

—Philippians 4:6 (NKJV)

We should always show gratitude for what God has given us. The more we show gratitude, the more God can bless us with more.

I am successful …

Commit to the Lord whatever you do, and
he will establish your plans.

—Proverbs 16:3 (NIV)

When we tell ourselves we are successful, we have no option
but to be. To be successful, you must be obedient.

I am confident ...

I can do all things through Christ who strengthens me.

—Philippians 4:13 (NKJV)

We are confident to do whatever we put our minds to do.

I am valuable ...

For I know the plans I have for you, declares the Lord, plans to prosper you and not to harm you, plans to give you hope and a future.

—Jeremiah 29:11 (NIV)

We are nothing without Jesus, but in and through Him, we are valuable and can do great things.

I am happy …

I know that there is nothing better for people than
to be happy and to do good while they live.

—Ecclesiastes 3:12 (NIV)

No matter what our situation or life looks like, we are
happy. We have the power to change how we feel.

I am wise ...

The wise prevail through great power, and those
who have knowledge muster their strength.

—Proverbs 24:5 (NIV)

We are wise through the wisdom God has given us.

I am healed ...

Lord my God, I called to you for help, and you healed me.

—Psalm 30:2 (NIV)

When we go to God in prayer regarding our sickness,
He can heal us. Nothing is too big for God.

I am healthy ...

For I will restore health to you and heal you
of your wounds, says the Lord.

—Jeremiah 30:17 (NKJV)

Our body belongs to God; therefore, we must take
care of His temple by what we feed it.

I am beautiful ...

You are altogether beautiful, my darling; there is no flaw in you.

—Song of Solomon 4:7 (NIV)

Every one of us is beautiful in the eyes of
God. Let no one tell you differently.

I am approved ...

If God is for us, who can be against us?
—Romans 8:31 (NKJV)

No matter who denies us, God will approve in His timing.

I am patient ...

And let us not be weary in well doing; for in due
season we shall reap, if we faint not.

—Galatians 6:9 (KJV)

In order for us to reap the blessings God has for
us, we must patiently wait on Him.

I am a better person ...

Create in me a clean heart, O God; and
renew a right spirit within in me.

—Psalm 51:10 (KJV)

When we make the decision to allow God to lead
and guide us, we become better women.

I am amazing …

I will praise You, for I am fearfully and wonderfully made;
Marvelous are your works, And that my soul knows very well.

—Psalm 139:14 (NKJV)

We all were wonderfully made in the eyes of God;
therefore, each of us is amazing in different ways.

I am free ...

So if the Son sets you free, you will be free indeed.

—John 8:36 (NIV)

We are free from bondage and burdens once we
place them at His feet. Let go, and let God.

I am not an overthinker …

Therefore, do not worry about tomorrow, for tomorrow will worry about itself. Each day has enough trouble of its own.

—Matthew 6:34 (NIV)

We must pray and ask God to declutter our wandering minds. The enemy tries to torment our minds; therefore, we must pull down every stronghold and plead the blood of Jesus.

I am abundant in all ways ...

Now unto him that is able to do exceeding abundantly above all
that we ask or think, according to the power that worketh in us.

—Ephesians 3:20 (KJV)

God will always exceed our expectations
when we trust Him with our lives.

I am creative ...

Therefore, if anyone is in Christ, the new creation
has come: The old has gone, the new is here!

—2 Corinthians 5:17 (NIV)

As long as we have a true relationship with God, we
can achieve anything we set our minds to do.

I am respected and respectful …

Do to others whatever you would like them to do to you.

—Matthew 7:12 (NLT)

We must give respect in order to get respect in return.

I am at peace with my past …

Peace I leave with you, My peace I give to you; not as the world gives do I give to you. Let not your heart be troubled, neither let it be afraid.

—John 14:27 (NKJV)

No matter what past hurts we have endured, we must place them at the feet of God and be willing to forgive ourselves as well as the person who hurt us.

I am fearfully made ...

No weapon formed against you shall prosper, And every tongue
which rises against you in judgement You shall condemn.

—Isaiah 54:17 (NKJV)

We should never live in fear. When we have a spirit of
fear in our lives, we will constantly be worried about what
might happen. We should always think positively.

I am prosperous ...

But seek ye first the kingdom of God, and his righteousness; and all these things shall be added unto you.

—Matthew 6:33 (KJV)

When we make God first in our life, everything we desire will be given unto us.

I am hopeful …

Now faith is the substance of things hoped
for, the evidence of things not seen.

—Hebrews 11:1 (KJV)

Although we cannot see the future, we must be
hopeful that God will supply all of our needs.

I am a giver ...

Give, and it will be given to you: good measure, pressed down,
shaken together, and running over will be put into your bosom.

—Luke 6:38 (NKJV)

When we give back to God what He has given to us,
we will never fall short. When we sow bountifully
to others, we will reap bountifully.

I am forgiving ...

If we confess our sins, He is faithful and just to forgive us
our sins, and to cleanse us from all unrighteousness.

—1 John 1:9 (KJV)

To truly live the life God has for us, we must forgive. In doing
so, we are moving forward and no longer looking in the past.

I am unstoppable ...

For nothing will be impossible with God.

—Luke 1:37 (CSB)

We can never be stopped as long as we have God with us.

I am loving and loved ...

We love because he first loved us.

—1 John 4:19 (NIV)

God loves us; therefore, we are loved and can give love to others.

I am worthy ...

She is clothed with strength and dignity, and
she laughs without fear of the future.

—Proverbs 31:25 (NLT)

We are worthy even when others tell us we are not.

I am motivated and determined ...

Be strong and courageous. Do not be afraid or terrified
because of them, for the Lord your God goes with
you; He will never leave you nor forsake you.

—Deuteronomy 31:6 (NIV)

When God has given us a vision to birth, we must be motivated
and determined to put in the work until it comes to fruition.

I am a positive thinker ...

Death and life are in the power of the tongue: and
they that love it shall eat the fruit thereof.

—Proverbs 18:21 (KJV)

When we change our mindset to things of positivity, we
will no longer allow negativity to come into our lives.

I am debt free ...

And forgive us our debts, as we forgive our debtors.

—Matthew 6:12 (NKJV)

When we repent of our sins, we are asking
God for a new and better life.

My Message to All Women

Always put God first before anyone or anything then take care of self. No matter how hard life gets, always remember to seek God, and allow Him to lead and guide you in every area of your life. God is intentional; He already knows what we want and need, but He wants us to come to Him and ask Him so He can supply our needs. Even if we have everything we need, we should always give Him thanks.

Having a relationship with God is a daily commitment that we must set aside time in our day to spend with Him. When we speak defeat, we will be defeated; therefore, we must change our mindset and make it a routine to speak life over every situation.

Our tongues have the power of life and death; therefore, we are what we speak. Some days may be harder than others, but push through until it becomes a habit. I promise if you start and end your day spending time with God, your life will change for the better. He has a plan for each of our lives, but we must seek Him diligently and allow Him to reveal His plan and purpose for our lives.

Ladies, with God all things are possible, and we have the power to accomplish anything.

When I made the decision to put God first in my life, everything started to work out for my good. There were times when the enemy tried to take over my mind and stop the blessings God had ordained for my life, but the enemy never wins. When we are children of the Most High God, nothing and nobody can stop things from manifesting in our lives. That is why it is so important for us to seek God daily by reading His word and devotionals, journaling, and just spending time in His presence. If we want everything God has for us, we must trust

Him with our lives and allow Him to lead and guide us in every area of our lives. I did not know anything about writing a book, but I love journaling. Therefore, I would always tell myself, "Write as if you are writing in your journal." I knew that I did not want to start something and not finish. God has done a new thing in my life, and He will do a new thing in your life also. Stepping out on faith is all it takes to step into the purpose God has for us.

I hope this book has encouraged you to change your mindset by speaking the affirmations daily. If anyone is questioning when they will have time to spend with God, my answer would be to wake up an hour before it is time to start your day. It can be done! I speak my affirmations over my life every morning in the car before I walk in to work. When doing these things, you are telling yourself you want to be the best version of yourself and you want everything you are speaking to come to fruition.

Once it becomes a habit in your life, you will find yourself helping someone else change his or her mindset. We will no longer allow the enemy to win by the words we speak, and by doing so, we will break off generational curses that have been passed down from generations before us. We have the power to change our situations, but it starts with us and the willingness to change.

I declare over each of your lives that after reading this book, *Nothing but Greatness*, your story and life will be changed for the better.

God bless.

I would love to hear your testimony. Feel free to email me at godsgrace8008@gmail.com.

Follow me on social media:

- @iamconstancenecole
- @Nothingbutgreatness8

Printed in the United States
by Baker & Taylor Publisher Services